Kung Fu

MARTIAL AND FIGHTING ARTS SERIES

Judo

Jujutsu

Karate

Kickboxing

Kung Fu

Martial Arts for Athletic Conditioning

Martial Arts for Children

Martial Arts for the Mind

Martial Arts for People with Disabilities

Martial Arts for Special Forces

Martial Arts for Women

Ninjutsu

Taekwondo

KUNG FU

NATHAN JOHNSON

Senior Consultant Editor
Aidan Trimble (6th Dan)
Former World, European, and
British Karate Champion
Chairman and Chief Instructor to the
Federation of Shotokan Karate

MASON CREST PUBLISHERS
www.masoncrest.com

Mason Crest Publishers Inc.
370 Reed Road
Broomall, PA, 19008
(866) MCP-BOOK (toll free)
www.masoncrest.com

First printing

1 2 3 4 5 6 7 8 9 10

Library of Congress Cataloging-in-Publication Data on file at the Library of Congress

ISBN 1-59084-393-2

Editorial and design by
Amber Books Ltd.
Bradley's Close
74–77 White Lion Street
London N1 9PF
www.amberbooks.co.uk

Project Editor Chris Stone
Design www.stylus-design.com
Picture Research Lisa Wren

Color reproduction by MRM Graphics, England
Printed and bound in Jordan

IMPORTANT NOTICE
The techniques and information described in this publication are for use in dire circumstances only where the safety of the individual is at risk. Accordingly, the publisher and copyright owner cannot accept any responsibility for any prosecution or proceedings brought or instituted against any person or body as a result of the use or misuse of the techniques and information within.

Picture Credits
Paul Clifton: 17, 18, 25, 33, 38, 54, 72, 85.
Nathan Johnson: 6, 11, 15, 29, 36, 43, 61, 62, 64, 65, 66.
The Picture Desk/Kobal: 8, 44, 69, 80, 87, 88.
Private Collection: 26, 82, 84.
Bob Willingham: 12, 75, 76.

Front cover image: Paul Clifton

Contents

Introduction

When I began studying the martial arts back in 1972, the whole subject was shrouded in mystery; indeed that was part of the attraction. At that time there was only a limited range of books on the subject and therefore very little information was available to the novice.

I am glad to say that this has in recent years changed beyond all recognition. With the explosion of interest in the martial arts and the vast array of quality books that are now on the market, we seem to be increasing our knowledge and understanding of the fighting arts and sports science and this fact is reflected in this new series of books.

Over the past thirty years I have been privileged to compete, train, and teach with practitioners from most of the disciplines covered in this series. I have coached world champions, developed and adapted training methods for people with disabilities, and instructed members of the armed forces in close-quarter techniques. I can warmly recommend this series as a rich source of information for student and instructor alike. Books can never replace a good instructor and club, but the student who does not study when the training is finished will never progress.

Aidan Trimble—Sixth Dan, Former World Karate Champion

Airborne kicking techniques, long a part of traditional Chinese theater, have found their way into kung fu and become an accepted and expected aspect of kung fu exhibitions.

What is Kung Fu?

Kung fu is a Cantonese Chinese word that can be roughly translated as "hard work." It is also a vulgar expression for an older term, wu shu (pronounced woo shoo). Wu shu is comprised of two Chinese ideograms, or characters, wu and shu, meaning "to stop or quell a spear." In this way, the term wu shu describes a Chinese form of martial arts.

While kung fu has been seen in films by millions of eager fans worldwide, kung fu as an activity has only become available to non-Chinese people in the past 40 years or so. An exciting and fascinating martial art, kung fu uses weapons as well as blocking, punching, striking, kicking, seizing, grappling, and throwing techniques.

Kung fu can be practiced in a group, with a friend—or even alone. It is suitable for all ages and levels of fitness and training, and can be customized to suit all individuals, including those with disabilities.

Most kung fu schools have a progressive curriculum, starting with the most basic techniques and working up to techniques that demand great skill. Kung fu can be practiced without equipment or a uniform. Very little space is needed, and techniques can be honed for as little as a few minutes at a time, or for as long as an hour or more. Kung fu is effective as an

The legendary Lee Jun-Fan, better known as Bruce Lee, the kung fu movie star, punched and kicked his way onto the big screen during the 1960s, and may well be the most famous kung fu movie star ever.

THE TRAINED MIND

"Monks, I know of no other single thing so conducive to misery as this uncultivated mind. Monks, I know of no other single thing so conducive to well-being as this cultivated and well-trained mind." —Anguttara Nikaya 1–6

exercise because it is balanced. Techniques are performed with both sides of the body, and the body is fully exercised because it is moved in all directions. Kung fu is a fascinating and progressive challenge—there is always something new to learn.

Practicing kung fu increases strength, coordination, agility, and flexibility. You can also expect to develop confidence, improve posture, and cultivate skill. In addition, kung fu fosters patience, tolerance, and understanding. Well-trained kung fu practitioners try their hardest to avoid actual fighting. In fact, in one kung fu film, Bruce Lee, the famous action-movie star, referred to his style as "the art of fighting without fighting."

A BIT OF HISTORY

The techniques that form the basis of kung fu supposedly originated in the Shaolin Temple, a Buddhist monastery in the Honan Province of China, although combative and self-defense techniques already existed in China

Right: Kung fu evolved from the Shaolin Temple, in Honan Province, China, where early practitioners modeled kung fu techniques on animal movements, like the white crane technique shown here.

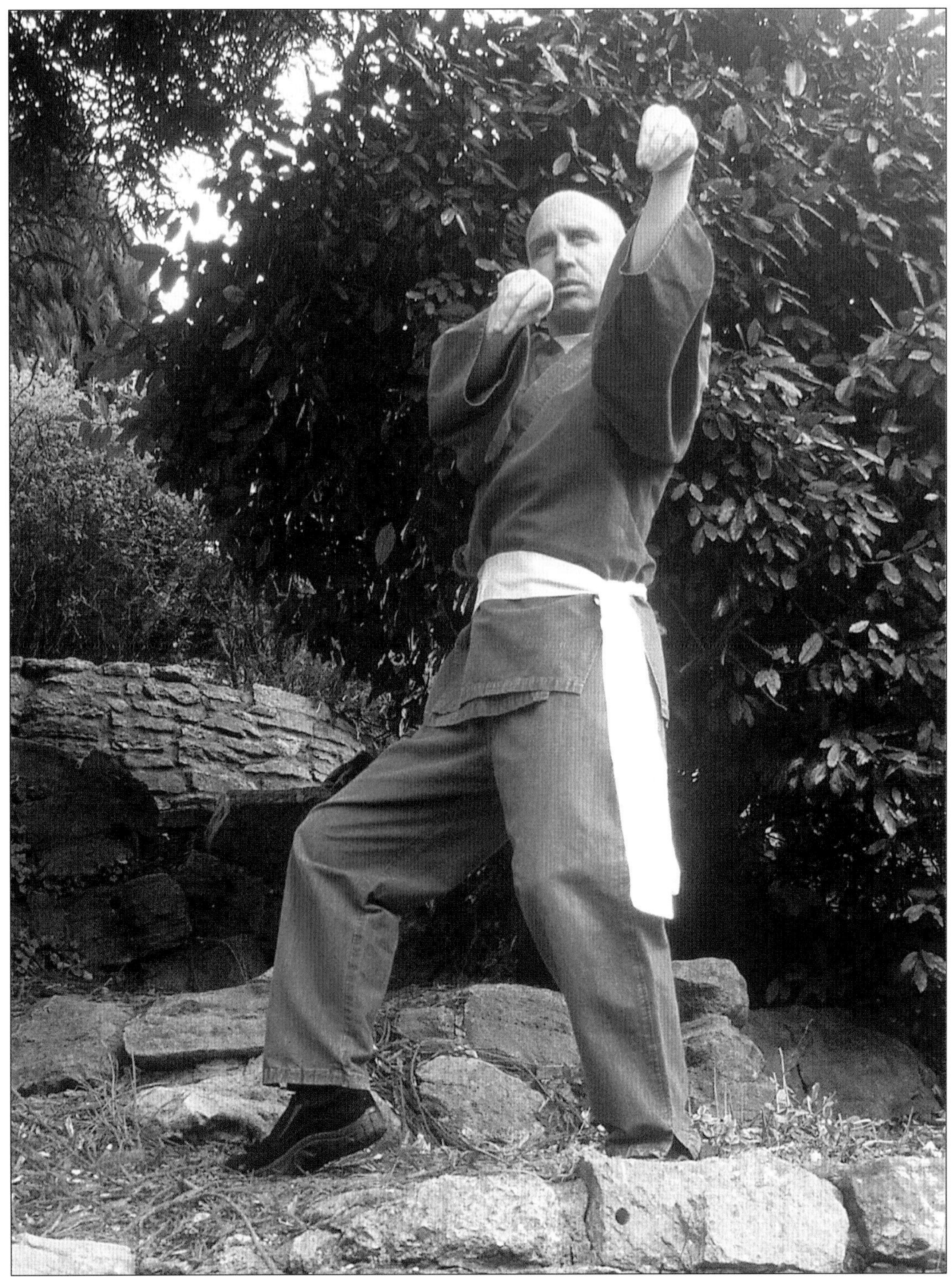

金棟健身社
CHEE KIM THONG
AND HEALTH SOCIETY

THE REAL VALUE OF KUNG FU

A peaceful mind is less inclined to fight and more inclined to enjoy life. Wan Lai Sheng, a famous kung fu master, was recorded as saying: "Do not ask me how I fight, I only do my (kung fu) exercises."

The real value of kung fu can be classified under the following:

- **Kung fu as a form of exercise.**
- **Kung fu as a form of self-defense.**
- **Kung fu as a form of self-discipline and spiritual training.**

before the founding of the temple. The Shaolin techniques stressed dignity and morality, and the Shaolin teachers were men and women of great integrity. The Ming Dynasty (1368–1644) was considered to be the golden era of kung fu.

Healing and self-defense techniques were popular in China from an early period. The techniques developed by the Chinese kung fu masters spread all over Asia, even finding a home on the Ryukyu (pronounced Reeyookoo) island of Okinawa, one of a small chain of islands roughly midway between China and Japan, where kung fu eventually developed into the art of karate. Today, both kung fu and karate are known virtually all over the world.

Left: For nearly 40 years, Oriental kung fu masters have increasingly and openly shared their knowledge with students from many countries, and these countries now boast their own masters of international standing.

THE VALUE OF KUNG FU

Kung fu is an art form. It is also a method of self-defense—not offense. There are many stories about the legendary power held by kung fu masters. It is useful to remember, however, that although hard training in kung fu brings skill and power, with that power comes responsibility—the responsibility not to be a show-off or a braggart and not to misuse your kung fu skills.

EXERCISE

Kung fu also has a long tradition of being used to entertain people. During the Ching Dynasty (1644–1911), medicine sellers would use kung fu to attract crowds. The martial arts book *Barefoot Zen* describes a staged fight between two medicine sellers:

"During the long journey from Sichuan to the misty peaks of Honan Province, Chu found that the food, language, customs, people, and villages varied considerably. In one village, the name of which he could not pronounce, he saw two medicine sellers fighting in the street. They growled at each other, leapt high into the air, clashed, and landed. One of them came down with a mock expression of pain on his face, and the other immediately

THE GREATER HAPPINESS

"If by renouncing a lesser happiness one attains to a happiness that is greater, then let the wise pursue that happiness which is greater." Dhammapada: 290

Outside training can be useful to help develop control and mastery of rough terrain, as this sidekick demonstrates.

JACKIE CHAN—MOVIE STAR

Jackie Chan, one of the most popular kung fu and action-movie stars in the world, studied for more than 10 years with Yu Chan-Yuan at the China Drama Academy. At the academy, a child would be put under a 10-year contract and drilled almost 24 hours a day in martial arts techniques, acrobatics, Peking opera, and mime, as well as academic subjects.

went on the offensive. The action was terrific: kicks, flips, dodges, punches, and counterpunches, all executed with precision and razor-sharp timing. It was amazing that neither of them got hurt! While the fight was in progress, a colleague of the two men (who was obviously their business partner) sold medicine to the crowd.

"When the fight was over, Chu ran over to the men, pretending not hear his uncle calling him back. 'How did you kick like that? Where did you learn? How did you know what to do? Are you hurt?' he blurted out. The grizzle-faced man who was the target of the questions merely smiled and winked at the boy before collecting a share of the medicine money and disappearing into the crowd."

This visually attractive, acrobatic kung fu style is the type of kung fu to which the general public has had the most exposure. However, the majority of traditional kung fu teachers do not consider kung fu's true purpose to be entertainment; the real value, they say, lies in its use as a form of self-defense.

High kicks are fun to do and can look impressive; however, they are not an essential element of conservative southern Shaolin kung fu.

SELF-DEFENSE

Kung fu has great value as a form of self-defense, but we must be guided by the wisdom and philosophy of the kung fu masters who have handed down the art of kung fu through the generations. If we ignore their philosophy, kung fu becomes nothing more than a way of brutalizing our fellow human beings. We will examine kung fu philosophy and how kung fu is used as a form of self and spiritual discipline later.

A NORTHERN-STYLE KICK

It is claimed that northern Chinese kung fu makes more widespread use of kicking techniques than the southern style, like this high-rising heel kick.

CHOOSING A STYLE

Traditional kung fu styles range from simple, direct, and economical (wing chun, for example) to incredibly complex, flowery, and expressive (cho lay fut, for example). There are also modern kung fu styles, the best known of which is probably Bruce Lee's jeet kune do style.

Left: Holding and hitting, seldom a part of sports fighting, are techniques featured prominently in the southern Chinese style of kung fu, where trapping and controlling limbs is an integral part of practice.

A SOUTHERN-STYLE FRONT KICK

STEP 1: Keeping your back straight and bending your "platform," or standing, leg, raise the knee of the kicking leg so it is parallel with the ground.

STEP 2: Thrust out and forward without making any special effort to straighten the leg. Keep the kick low, and strike using the heel.

Despite the large range of kung fu styles, kung fu (like karate) can be roughly divided into two basic approaches: traditional kung fu, which is studied as both a fighting method and an art form, and sport kung fu. Other methods of classifying kung fu styles are: north, south, hard, and soft.

NORTHERN AND SOUTHERN STYLES

Kung fu is often divided into northern and southern styles. Northern styles typically use large, expansive movements; wide stances; and lots of kicks, particularly high ones. Southern styles use small, direct, economical movements; high, narrow stances; and only a few low kicks.

Personally, I am not convinced by these somewhat outdated and inaccurate classifications. These misconceptions go back to 1911 when kung fu had already lost much of its vitality and importance in Chinese society. By then, kung fu styles had spread out and changed or developed at great speed and things got mixed up. For example, hung gar and cho lay fut, two popular kung fu styles (classified as southern) make extensive use of the legs for kicking, and use wide open stances, as does the allegedly southern tam tui, or "deep legs" style. Pa-kua chang kung fu, however—supposedly from the north—uses narrow stances and employs few (if any) kicks.

CHOOSING A KUNG FU STYLE

It is sometimes best to ignore these kung fu classifications (as they can be quite confusing) and concentrate on simply finding a style that is best for you. We are all different, and we will all take differing attitudes, physiques, levels of flexibility, hand–eye coordination abilities, and a whole host of other factors into the kung fu training hall. If you decide to train in kung fu, look for a club or a teacher. So long as the tuition is reasonable and professional, and so long as you like what you see, go for it.

A NORTHERN-STYLE KICK

Stand in a ready position, with your feet a little more than shoulder-width apart, relax your shoulders, hold your clenched fists in front of and away from your body, and keep the elbows slightly bent. To perform the kick, raise your knee. Kick forward, outward, and upward, making sure to keep the heel of your supporting leg firmly on the ground. Both the toes and the ball of the foot—and occasionally the heel—are used to make contact with the intended target.

A SOUTHERN-STYLE FRONT KICK

Stand in a ready position. Raise your knee. Kick forward, turning your foot outward as you kick. The heel is the part of the foot that makes contact with the target.

HARD AND SOFT STYLES

Although a controversial method of classification, some divide kung fu styles into hard or soft. Hard styles are said to be rigid, jerky, crude, and confrontational; while soft styles are said to be subtle, flowing, yielding, pliant, and skillful.

This method of classification is not exactly accurate, however, in that there are many exceptions to these rules. For example, tai chi chuan ("grand ultimate fist"), a so-called soft kung fu style (see page 39), is usually seen as a soft, slow, tranquil sort of exercise. However, tai chi chuan has a method of issuing energy that is just as explosive or dynamic as that found in so-called hard kung fu styles. Similarly, many so-called hard styles use plenty of circular and flowing movements (usually attributed to soft styles), as well as "listening" techniques. Listening techniques are dependent on the sense of touch; they are used to read and determine an opponent's strength and to determine the nature and direction of an attack—hardly the practice of a muscle-bound, hard-style practitioner.

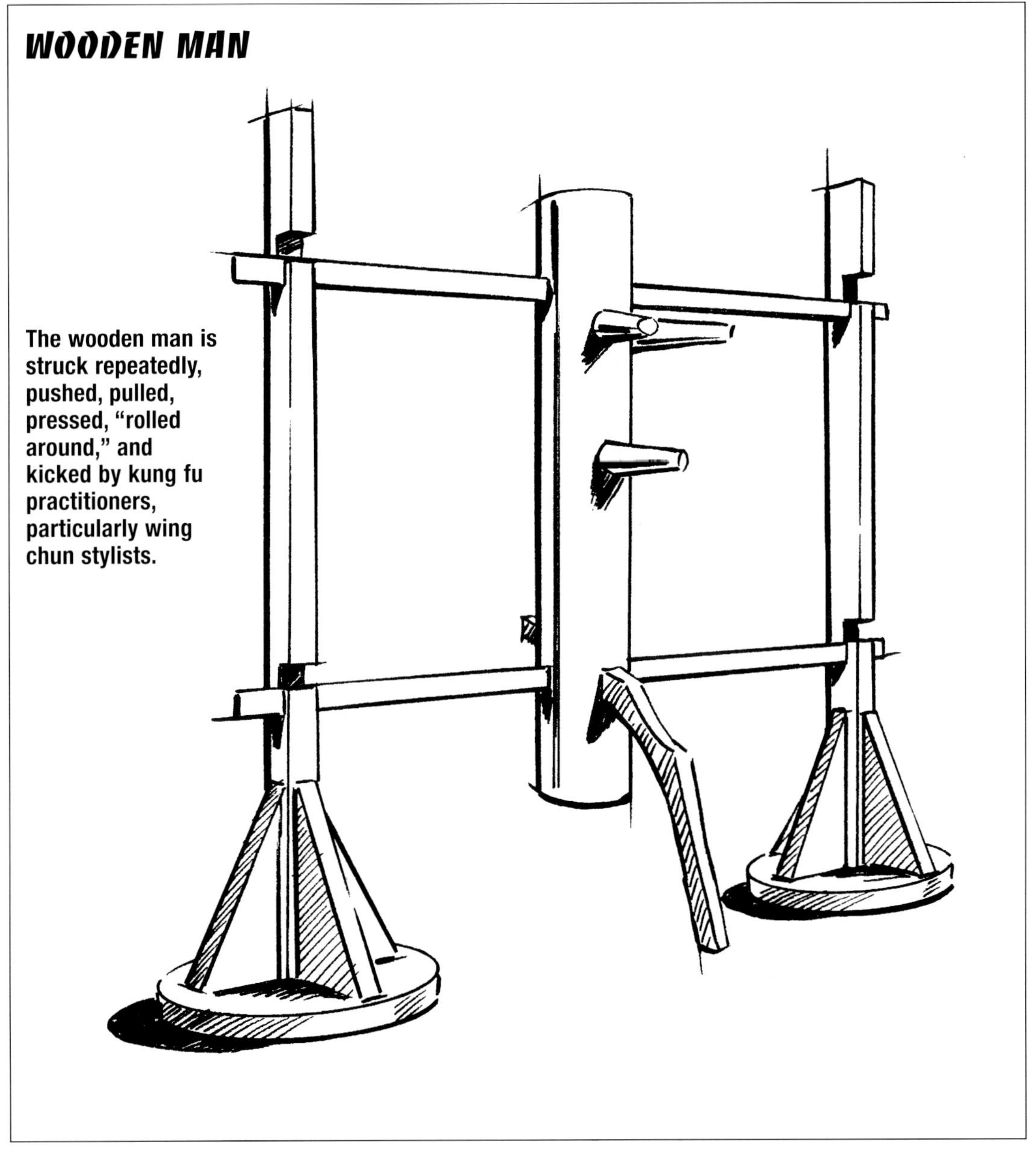

The wooden man is struck repeatedly, pushed, pulled, pressed, "rolled around," and kicked by kung fu practitioners, particularly wing chun stylists.

POPULAR KUNG FU STYLES

Below are 10 of the most popular and well-known kung fu styles. You may come across some of them if you decide to join a kung fu class.

WHITE CRANE

Origin: From the Fukien Province in China, **white crane** is a general term used to describe southern Shaolin-based kung fu.

Description: White crane uses short, narrow stances. It is made up primarily of hand techniques, and the few kicks it uses are kept low. White crane has a number of related systems with exotic names, like flying crane, feeding crane, and singing crane. White crane (like certain types of karate) often begins training with a form (**kata** in Japanese) called sanchin or saamchien, which means "three conflicts."

WING CHUN

Origin: A famous and popular style of kung fu, wing chun has its origins in the Shaolin kung fu of a Buddhist nun called Ng Mui (pronounced Oong Moy). History (or legend) claims that Ng Mui taught her system to a young woman called Yim Wing Chun, who then gave her name to the style.

Description: Wing chun has a compact, economical, close-quarters style, with few kicking techniques. Any kicks in wing chun are kept low, with the shins, knees, and thighs among the targets. Wing chun is often characterized by a no-nonsense, straight-line approach, particularly in its punching techniques, in which a rapid burst of connected straight-line punches are fired down an imaginary center line directly at an opponent. Wing chun practices three **tao-kuen** (fist forms). Wing chun also practices a set of techniques used in conjunction with a "wooden man." The wooden man is a post with wooden pegs sticking out of it to represent arms and one leg. It is struck and kicked by the practitioner.

PAK MEI

Origin: This style was created by the monk Bak Mei Too Jung, who belonged to the famed Shaolin Temple.

Description: Pak mei, like wing chun, is a compact, close-quarters style of kung fu, with few kicking techniques. Pak mei students often begin training

Bruce Lee once said: "What's practical on the street isn't spectacular in the movies, and what's spectacular in the movies isn't practical on the streets." Practical and spectacular techniques both have their place in contemporary kung fu.

with a form called gow bow tui, meaning "nine-step push." This form has many similarities to the sanchin form of the white crane style.

MONKEY STYLE

Origin: This kung fu style was inspired by the heroic actions of China's legendary Monkey King, a mythical figure from Chinese history and a formidable warrior.

Description: The monkey style is a type of kung fu known as "animal-imitating kung fu." This kung fu style combines the techniques of attack

Kung fu posters, like this, have begun to form an integral part of kung fu iconography, and early posters from as late as the 1960s are traded by collectors. This one shows monkey-style kung fu.

and defense, such as kicking, striking, holding, throwing, leaping, and somersaulting. It also incorporates quick, nimble responses that mimic the actions of a monkey.

CHOY LAY FUT

Origin: 17th century.

Description: Choy lay fut kung fu is composed of three elements: the choy family of kung fu; the lay, or li, family of kung fu; and **buddha-hand** kung fu. Choy lay fut uses expansive circular arcing and swinging techniques, as well as open-hand techniques, backfist techniques, and elbow techniques. Kicking techniques are limited in choy lay fut; those that exist are sometimes aimed at high targets (this may be due to modern influences).

HUNG GAR

Origin: 17th century.

Description: Hung gar means "hung family." It is based on the five animal techniques, or forms, of Shaolin kung fu: snake, tiger, dragon, leopard, and crane. The movements of hung gar kung fu are generally dynamic and flowery, but they are also forceful, direct, and practical. While some styles use tricks to beat an opponent, hung gar kung fu relies on stability, speed, and power.

HUNG KUEN

Origin: 17th century.

Description: Hung kuen means "hung fist." It is similar to the hung gar style, but the extent to which this is so will depend on the teacher.

PRAYING MANTIS

Origin: Allegedly created by the 17th-century monk, Wang Lang. **Description:** Praying mantis kung fu has two basic branches: northern and southern. The praying mantis is an insect that grasps its prey with powerful pincer movements. It does not let go, even if it is cut in half. It is an apt name for this particular style of kung fu, which involves grabbing, holding, and then striking. Originally, praying mantis kung fu had only one form, but today, some modern praying mantis styles have 50 forms or more.

PA-KUA

Origin: Tung Hai-Chuan of Hopeh Province learned the art from an anonymous Taoist during the Ching Dynasty (1798–1879).

Description: Pa-kua is Chinese for "eight directions." This type of kung fu has a smooth, flowing style that makes extensive use of a technique called "walking," or "turning," the circle.

One of the major tactics in this style is to reposition yourself away from your opponent—moving to the side, or even behind, him or her—while neutralizing his or her limbs.

JEET KUNE DO

Origin: Bruce Lee, the Chinese martial artist and movie star, created jeet kune do.

Right: Proper warm-up is necessary prior to engaging in any martial art. The body should be both warmed up and warmed down after training to minimize cramps, muscle fatigue, and the "wear and tear" of a workout.

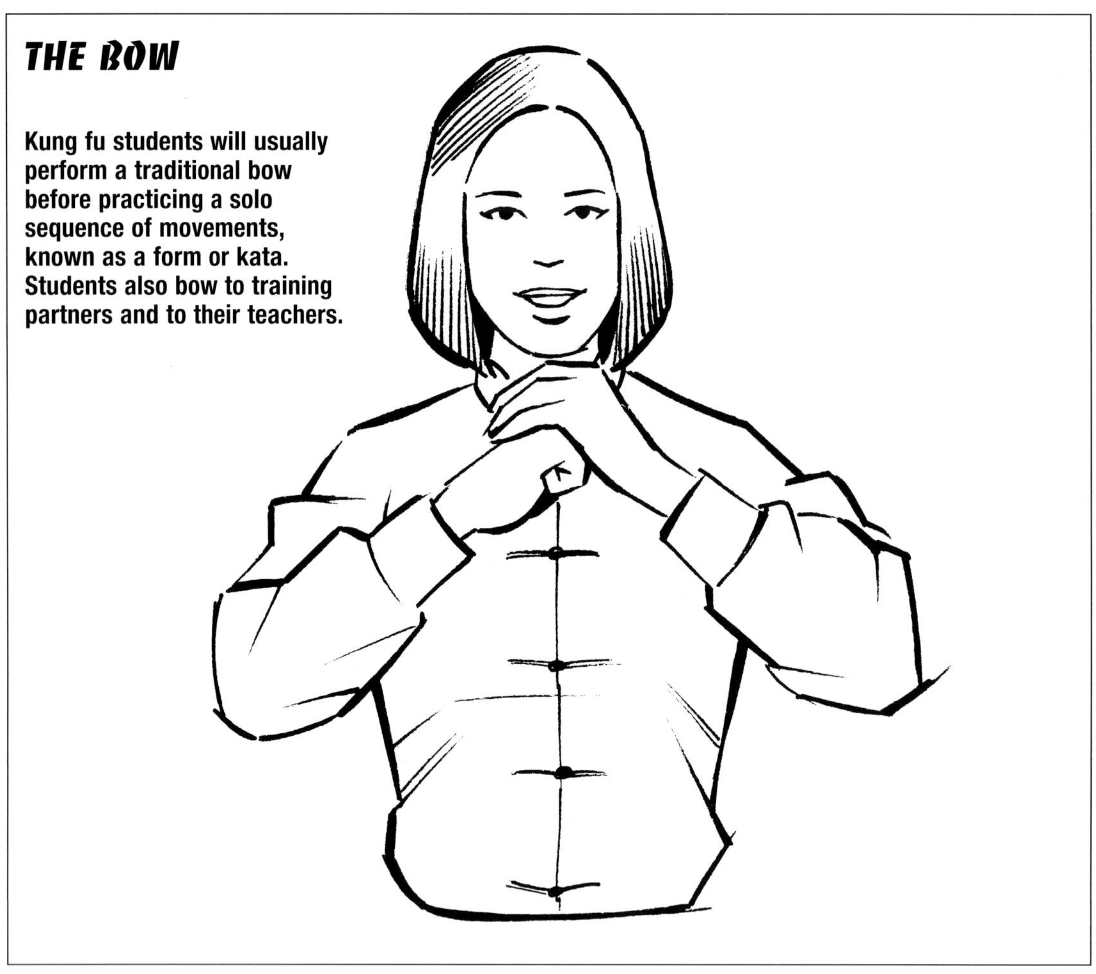

THE BOW
Kung fu students will usually perform a traditional bow before practicing a solo sequence of movements, known as a form or kata. Students also bow to training partners and to their teachers.

Description: Jeet kune do means: "the way of the intercepting fist." Lee created jeet kune do as a form of practical fighting for a modern era. As such, this style of kung fu dispenses with most of the traditional values, ideas, practices, and techniques of classical kung fu.

This does not necessarily make jeet kune do better or worse than other, more-traditional kung fu styles; it just makes it different from them. In fact, it is so different in style from classical or traditional kung fu styles that it really cannot be compared with them.

GETTING STARTED

We will now take a look at the preparation required to make kung fu practice safe, enjoyable, and productive.

THE KUNG FU UNIFORM

Most traditional kung fu schools encourage students to obtain and wear a uniform for training. Traditionally, this is a loose-fitting, black, two-piece set consisting of pants and a jacket. Less-traditional schools use colored uniforms, tracksuits, or even t-shirts. One of the benefits of wearing a uniform is that it makes everybody appear more or less the same—there is no hierarchy in kung fu. Some kung fu schools also use footwear, ranging from Chinese cotton slippers to running shoes. Other schools train barefoot.

Students should be encouraged to keep their uniforms clean, to keep fingernails and toenails short, and to remove (or cover with tape) all jewelry to avoid scratching others. The kung fu uniform is often tied with a colored sash that can denote the rank or grade of an individual. In kung fu, there are many different ranking systems, but an increasing number of schools are now following the ranking systems similar to those found in **judo** and **karate**. However, some kung fu schools have no ranks or grades at all.

It should always be remembered that kung fu skills themselves are much more important than the uniform you wear or the rank you hold, which, after all, are only a means to an end. Training alone in your home, your yard, or the park can be just fine. In fact, many kung fu practitioners train in their everyday clothes.

TRAINING

Before starting to train in kung fu, most modern practitioners warm up, gently stretching and exercising the body in order to avoid strains, muscle pulls, or other injuries. The old kung fu schools tended to use the kung fu itself as an exercise. Even today one can see people in public parks all over China, Taiwan, and Hong Kong using various kung fu styles as a means to get a little exercise and keep fit. Basic warm-up movements may include push-ups, sit-ups, the triceps stretch, rotating the arms, rotating the waist, squatting on the heels, stretching the hamstrings, and sitting with the soles of the feet pressed together and pushing the knees to the floor (known as the butterfly).

Modern kung fu training is usually divided into three basic categories: forms, applications, and sparring (or pushing- and **sticking-hands**). Sparring is a modern invention, born of competitive martial arts.

STANCES

Fundamental to all categories of kung fu training is posture, or stance. Kung fu stances should provide stability and balance for blocking, punching, striking, kicking, grappling, locking, and using weapons, but they must also allow for flexibility and mobility. Most traditional southern Chinese kung fu stances operate within the natural range of movement, a point supported by the findings of the sports manufacturing company, Reebok, which investigated the safest maximum degree of knee bend permissable for safety in sport and exercise. This angle was reported as being 60 degrees on the back of the knee, the angle traditionally found in kung fu stances.

The following paragraphs describe some of the most important and well-used kung fu stances.

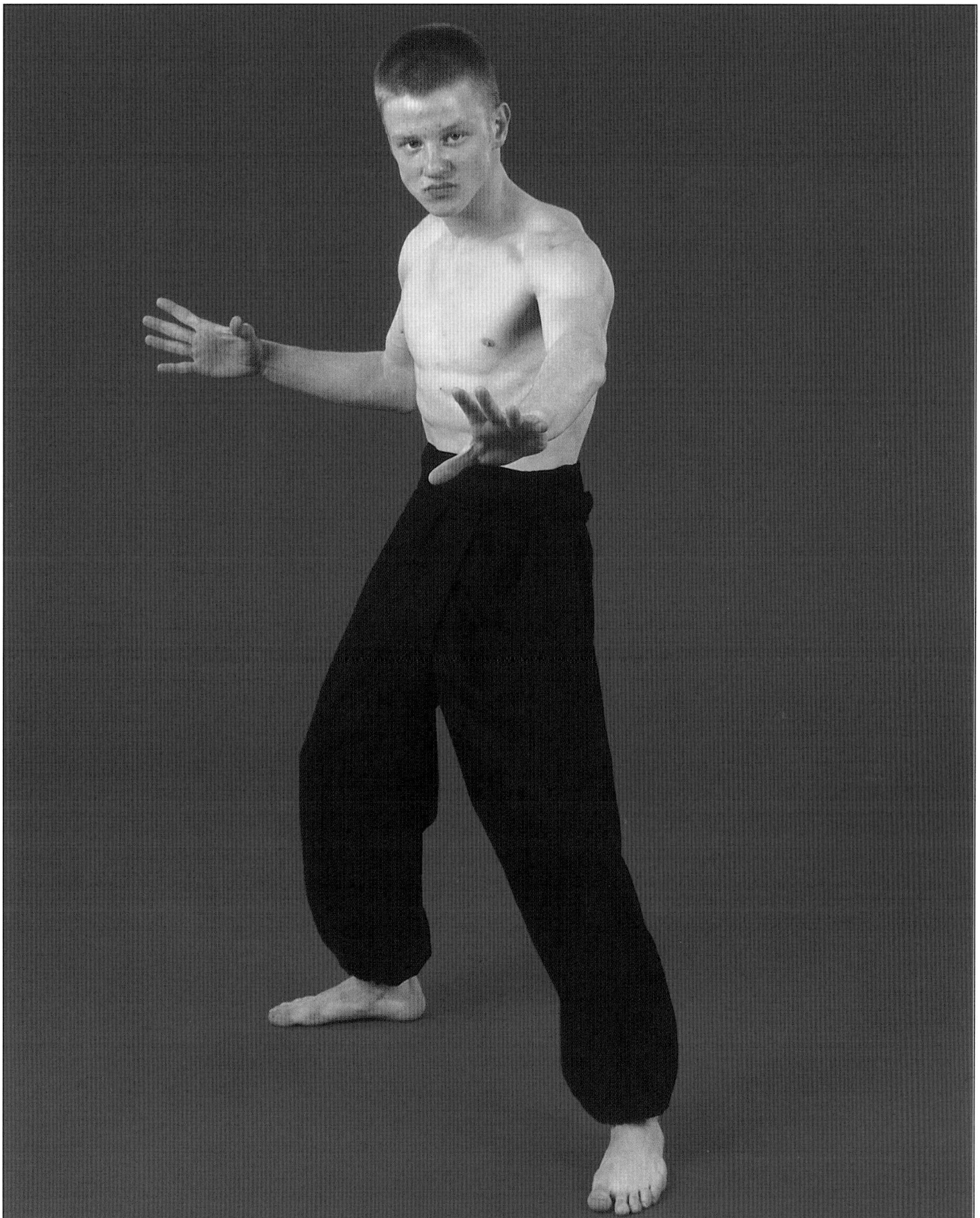

The late kung fu movie star, Bruce Lee, pioneered nonconventional and dramatic poses like this one.

STANCES

HORSE STANCE:
Making sure your back is straight, bend your knees so that your thighs are between 45 and 85 degrees. Relax your shoulders and breathe naturally.

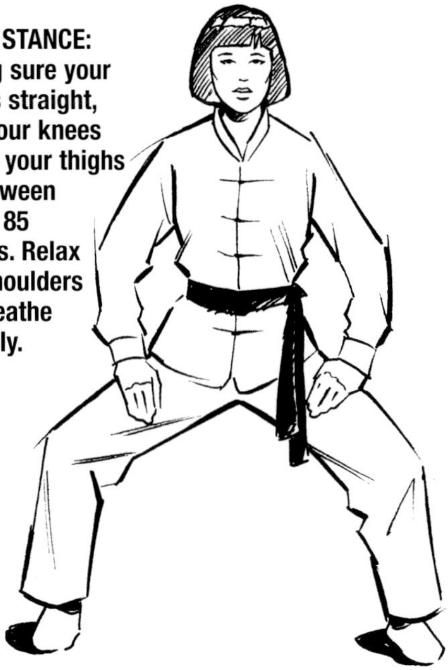

FRONT STANCE:
Keeping your back straight, bend your front leg and straighten your back leg to form this stance. Ensure your shoulders are down and remain equally balanced.

BACK STANCE:
To form the back stance, make sure that your center of gravity is shifted away from your extended front leg.

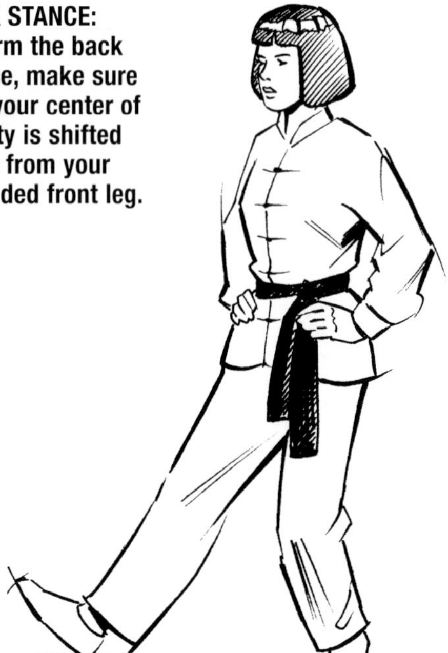

CAT STANCE:
To assume the cat stance, shift your weight to the rear as you did for the back stance, except this time, bend the front leg and position the front foot so that only the ball of the foot rests on the ground.

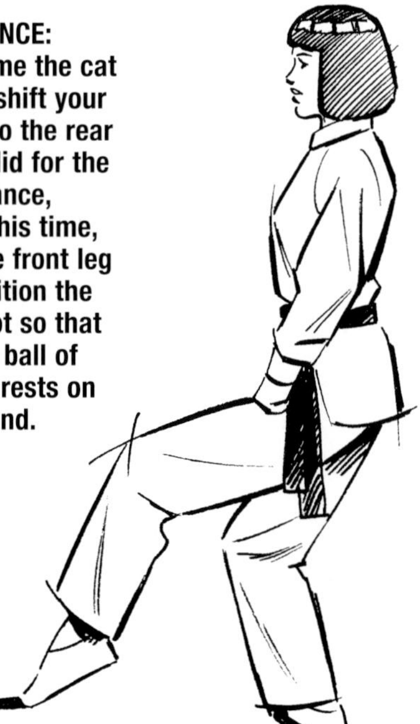

HORSE STANCE

The most traditional of all kung fu stances is the "horse-riding," or "horse," stance. It has many variations in foot placement, as well as in height and angle of the knees, but it is considered to be the fundamental kung fu stance. The horse stance was traditionally considered so important that, some years ago, students of Shaolin kung fu would practice nothing but the horse stance daily for more than six months.

To practice the horse stance, stand with your feet approximately one and a half shoulder-widths apart, bend your knees, and turn your feet in. Grip the ground with your feet, and let your hips fall into a natural position. Keep your shoulders down and square. This is a good stance to use when engaged in seizing and grappling techniques, as it is strong against both pushes and pulls.

FRONT STANCE

Stretch your back leg fully straight. Bend your front leg until your knee makes a vertical line with your toes. Keep your hips balanced. This is a good stance for both offense and defense.

BACK STANCE

Extend your front leg, and bend your rear leg, supporting about 70 percent of your weight on it. This stance is primarily used for defense.

CAT STANCE

The cat stance is a narrower version of the back stance. Stand with your back leg bent and supporting about 90 percent of your weight. Place your front leg so that only the ball of your foot touches the ground.

Shaolin Kung Fu

The Shaolin Temple, located in Honan Province, China, is the traditional home of kung fu. In fact, most Oriental styles trace their origins, however distant, back to the Shaolin Temple. Jou Tsung Hwa, a prominent writer and teacher of tai chi chuan, informs us that: "All the styles, names, and clans of Chinese martial arts are generated from Shaolin Chuan (Shaolin fist), the prototypical Chinese martial art."
***The Tao of Tai Chi,* Tuttle, 1980**

KUNG FU PHILOSOPHY

Kung fu supposedly spread from the Shaolin Temple, and so it is useful to look to the temple for an understanding of kung fu philosophy, beliefs, and ideals.

Kung fu is often associated with the ancient wisdom of China. The sources of this wisdom come from Taoism, Confucianism, and Chan (Zen) Buddhism. In ancient China, when a student began training in kung fu, he or she was usually "adopted" or taken on by a **sifu** (pronounced seefoo), meaning "father-teacher." This is the traditional Chinese relationship between master and student. No matter how good the student becomes, the student-teacher relationship will always remain the same.

"Sticking-hands" has always been an integral part of kung fu techniques that operate by "touch reflex." Such reflexes bypass the "seeing, thinking" mind and are therefore instantaneous.

"All the anger that you hold is like holding a red-hot iron ball with which you threaten everybody. All the time you hold it, you burn only yourself. All power is limited except wisdom, and the highest wisdom is love."

When a kung fu practitioner trains with a teacher, that teacher is not only able to correct physical details. The teacher can also monitor the state of mind that governs how the student flows from one technique to another; how the student absorbs, borrows, and returns an opponent's force; and whether the student can flow with an opponent's movements.

Using the correct methods, the student will learn to remain calm under pressure and to rise above fear, violence, and insecurity. Physical proficiency is a reflection of the state of mind of the kung fu practitioner.

There is much more to kung fu than mere fighting. Indeed, the so-called fighting skill that can be gained by practicing kung fu is only a by-product of the skills acquired in mastering ourselves. Serious practitioners of the art do not invest a lot of time and energy preparing for a fight they may never have. Kung fu philosophy seeks to remove fear and aggression in an individual, and kung fu practitioners do not encourage violence in thought, word, or deed.

Serious kung fu practitioners believe that fighting is an animal instinct and, therefore, to fight is to become an animal. In contrast, the kung fu master always appears to be dignified, upright, and civilized. He or she is never a thug or a bully and is most reluctant (outside of the practice hall) to use the very skills for which he or she is noted.

THE ART OF TAI CHI CHUAN

Although tai chi chuan (commonly known as tai chi) is not usually considered a style of kung fu, many kung fu practitioners practice it as well. Tai chi chuan translates as "grand ultimate fist." People all over the world practice it on a daily basis. It can be performed alone or in a group, and is practiced in a long, slow, choreographed sequence of gentle movements. At first sight, it appears that kung fu and tai chi chuan are quite different, but some believe that Chang San Feng, the legendary creator of tai chi, reworked original Shaolin kung fu forms to create tai chi.

THE FIVE ANIMALS

The original Shaolin kung fu was said to be based around five animals: snake, tiger, leopard, crane, and dragon. Each animal was meant to represent a certain type of movement and energy, such as fierceness (the tiger), grace (the crane), and stealth (the snake). Each animal could also be represented using a hand position, and thus there is a snake hand position, a tiger claw position, a crane beak position, a leopard claw position, and long and short dragon claw positions. The crane style is the most prominent among the styles of kung fu.

WHITE CRANE KUNG FU

In China, white crane kung fu is known by three separate names in Mandarin and Cantonese Chinese alone. In Mandarin, it is known as pai ho; in Cantonese, it is known both as pak hoc and peh ho.

White Crane is not really one particular kung fu style; rather, it is a combination of several styles. There are three major types of white crane kung fu styles: Fukien white crane (ying tsun peh ho), Tibetan lama white crane (si chang lama pai ho), and the techniques of the tiger-crane style (hung chia).

STAY IN CONTROL

"He who controls his rising anger as a skilled driver curbs a rolling chariot, him I call a true charioteer. Others merely hold the reins."
Dhammapada, Canto XVI

THE FIVE ANIMALS

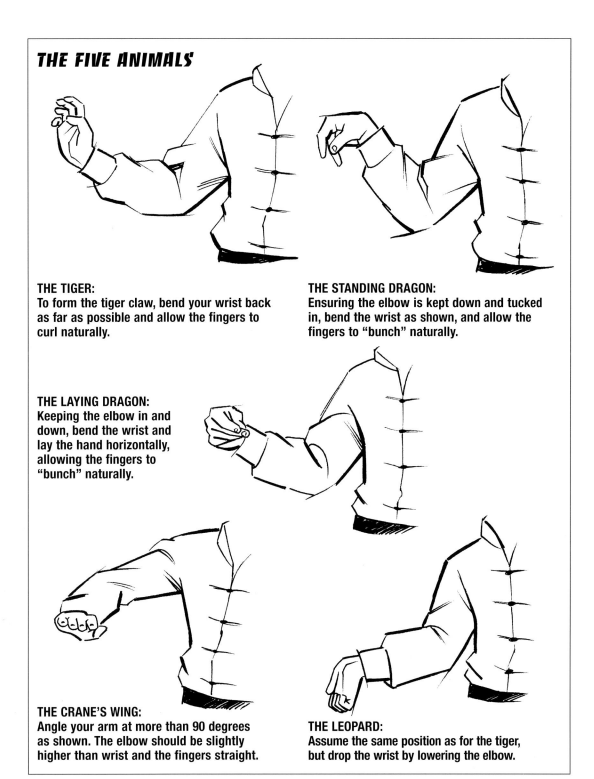

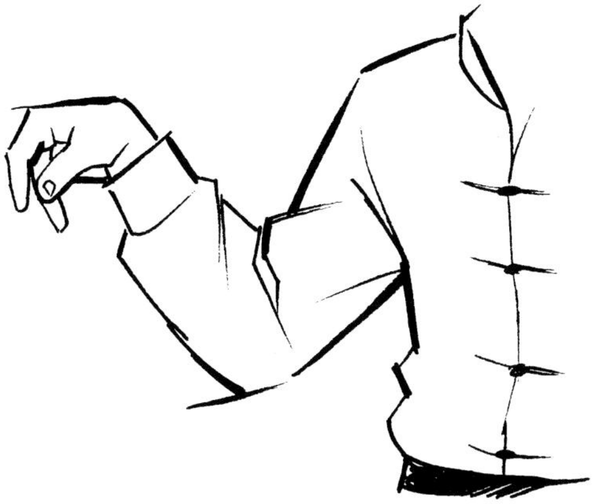

THE TIGER:
To form the tiger claw, bend your wrist back as far as possible and allow the fingers to curl naturally.

THE STANDING DRAGON:
Ensuring the elbow is kept down and tucked in, bend the wrist as shown, and allow the fingers to "bunch" naturally.

THE LAYING DRAGON:
Keeping the elbow in and down, bend the wrist and lay the hand horizontally, allowing the fingers to "bunch" naturally.

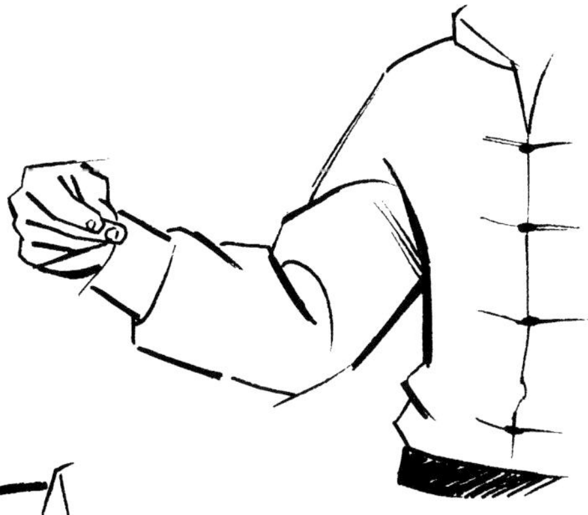

THE CRANE'S WING:
Angle your arm at more than 90 degrees as shown. The elbow should be slightly higher than wrist and the fingers straight.

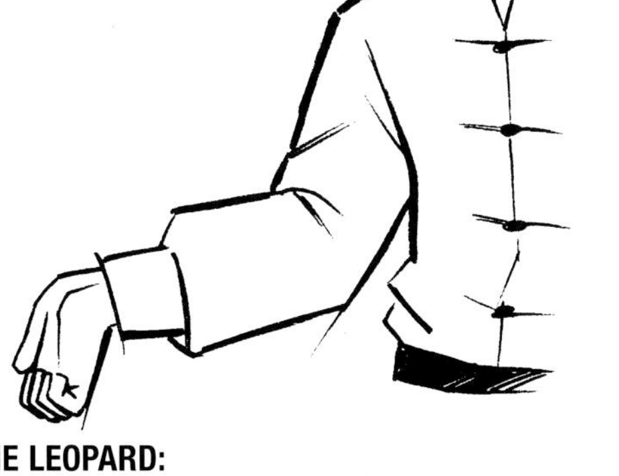

THE LEOPARD:
Assume the same position as for the tiger, but drop the wrist by lowering the elbow.

THE MYTH OF THE WHITE CRANE

A legendary fight between a snake and a crane appears in a story about the alleged founder of tai chi chuan, the Taoist monk Chang San Feng. History also recounts a similar tale concerning the founding of wing chun kung fu; its founder was also supposed to have been inspired by a fight between a snake and a crane.

FUKIEN WHITE CRANE

Fukien white crane kung fu was founded by Fang Chi-Liang. It uses short hand movements and emphasizes the development of "internal" power, or **chi**. One of the guiding principles of this style is "rising-falling," or attack and retract. In practice, the opponent's attack is "sucked in"; its force is made use of; and then it is "spat out." The Chinese refer to this sequence as float, sink, swallow, and spit.

TIBETAN LAMA WHITE CRANE

A Chinese wrestler named Hoh Ta Toh founded Tibetan lama white crane in 14th-century Tibet. According to legend, Hoh Ta Toh was meditating, when all of a sudden, he noticed that a large white crane (a bird with an elegant neck and a long beak) was engaged in a struggle with a large ape. Toh was amazed that the bird was able to fend off the attacks of the ape.

Right: Some kung fu techniques, like the flying-fingers strike shown opposite, were once considered "secret" and were traditionally withheld from the general syllabus. Recently, such techniques have become mainstream.

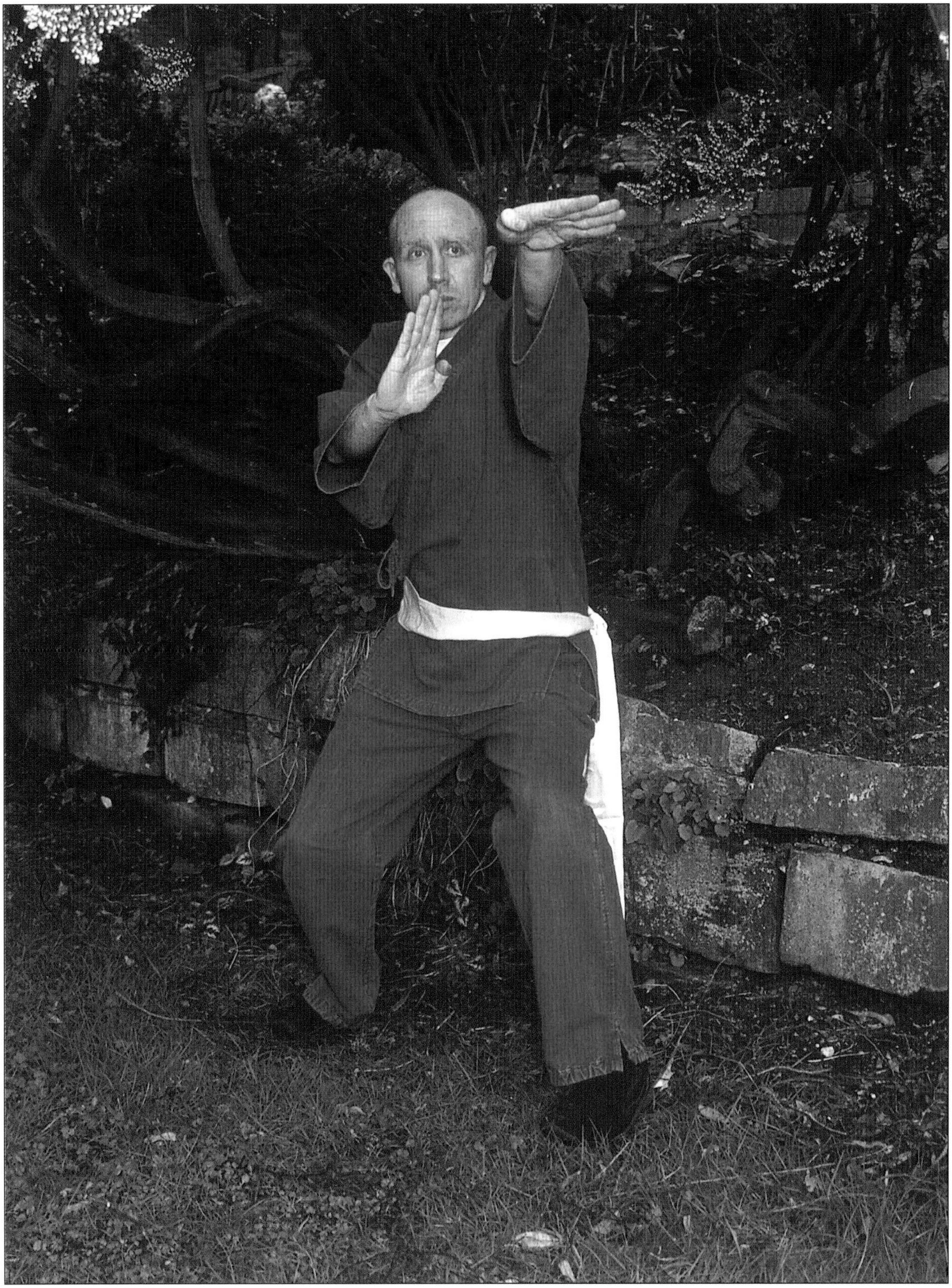

Legend has it that this encounter prompted Toh to copy the movements of the crane.

Tibetan lama white crane uses large, long, sweeping arm movements together with continuous circling movements that imitate the flapping of a crane's wings. Opponents find it difficult to penetrate the continuously rotating fists, finger jabs, and palm strikes.

Kung fu movie star Bruce Lee captivated audiences with his electrifying screen performances. One of his favorite film themes insisted on the superiority of kung fu over karate. In reality, however, individual skill always counts more than the style.

WHITE CRANE TECHNIQUES

Aside from the three major white crane styles, many kung fu styles originated in—or were influenced by—white crane techniques and principles. Choy lay fut (see page 27), for instance, has a white crane form; tai chi chuan also has movements styled after the white crane.

TIGER-CRANE (HUNG CHIA)

The Hung family, a prominent Chinese kung fu family, allegedly created the tiger-crane style. This style actually combines the techniques of the five animal forms of Shaolin kung fu (see page 40). Of these five forms, tiger-crane became the most widely known, thus giving the style its name. Tiger-crane techniques are exotic and attractive, but they are also practical.

WING CHUN KUNG FU

Roughly translated, wing chun means "beautiful springtime." The main reason that wing chun has become so popular is that it is the kung fu style formerly studied by the film star Bruce Lee. Lee received tuition from Yip Man, the Grand Master of wing chun, and some of his senior students, notably Wong Sheun Leung and William Cheung.

Wing chun is a direct, simple, no-nonsense kung fu style with no frills or showy techniques. It is concise, precise, compact, and economical, and is usually applied at great speed. One hallmark of wing chun is that it blocks and counterattacks at the same time.

All wing chun techniques operate within the natural range of movement, so flexibility is relatively unimportant. There are few leg techniques; when the leg is used, however, kicks, foot blocks, foot-sweeps, and traps are kept low and are supported by hand techniques. A wing chun stylist will usually already be in contact with an opponent before using a leg technique. "Kick with three legs on the ground" is a well-known wing chun motto. It means that a wing chun stylist should preferably kick while already holding an opponent.

JEET KUNE DO

Jeet kune do is the kung fu style created by Bruce Lee, the aforementioned famous film star. According to Danny Inosanto, a former student of Lee's, 50 percent of jeet kune do is founded on wing chun. But, as Inosanto said in reference to Lee and jeet kune do: "Its roots are founded on wing chun, but he [Bruce] went out of it…[departed from pure wing chun]."

Lee combined wing chun with whatever he thought was appropriate at a given time. Using a process of trial and elimination, he came up with a modern, nontraditional type of kung fu. Lee encouraged his students to, in his words, "absorb what is useful and reject what is useless."

There are no forms or fixed patterns of movement in jeet kune do. There are, however, lots of Western boxing and wrestling techniques. Surprisingly, given Lee's screen image, there are no high kicks in jeet kune do proper. As Lee said: "What's spectacular for a movie is not practical on the street."

Lee devised individual training routines or programs for his students, depending on their strengths and weaknesses. Some students were given

WHITE CRANE TECHNIQUES

LEFT: This pecking crane technique represents a popular but thoroughly modern example of white crane kung fu.

ABOVE: Here, two fighters assume ritual positions and prepare for contact.

LEFT: The attacker's "vertical"* punch is parried with the hooking action of the crane's beak. Counter-attack is either simultaneous or follows in an instant.

***(Little finger edge of the fist pointing down.)**

flexibility exercises to work on, while others were given strength-building exercises.

Lee also developed a wide variety of training devices for hand and foot conditioning to toughen them up so that they could withstand more impact. He used a punching and kicking bag that was suspended from both the floor and the ceiling, and devised and used padded focus gloves—gloves that protect the hand against injury when using a punching bag.

WING CHUN PALM-HAND BLOCK AND COUNTER

STEP 1: Shifting your body to the side, extend your open, palm-up hand to intercept your opponent's attack.

STEP 2: Blocking hand in place, counter-attack to your opponent's midsection using a "vertical"* punch

***(Little finger edge of the fist pointing down.)**

STICKING-HANDS

Both defensive and offensive techniques are triggered by contact with the opponent—and not merely by what you see him or her doing. During an attack, changes in circumstance are read automatically by the arms, which, acting like the antennae of an insect, remain in contact with your opponent's arms and detect every movement. In wing chun kung fu, this is called "sticking-hands."

Despite the heavy emphasis that Lee seems to have placed on combat efficiency, the kung fu magazine *Inside Kung Fu* reported him as saying, "Life is combat…a punch or a kick is not to knock the hell out of the guy in front, but to knock the hell out of your ego, your fears, or your hang-ups." From this quote, we can see that despite Lee's apparent divergence from traditional kung fu, his bottom-line philosophy is remarkably traditional.

BLOCKING TECHNIQUES

Avoiding, checking, and deflecting are the best ways to prevent an opponent's attack from causing you harm. Kung fu offers many ways to achieve these goals.

WHITE CRANE HOOKING BLOCK AND COUNTER

Starting in a ready stance, move to the side as your opponent steps in to attack. Using the crane's beak (bunching your fingertips together in a shape reminiscent of a crane's beak), deflect the blow aside as you "turn" your opponent's corner. You may choose to follow up with a crane strike as a counterattack.

WING CHUN SIMULTANEOUS ATTACK AND DEFENSE

Stand in the wing chun ready position. Move to the side as your opponent steps in to attack, and deflect the attack with a palm-hand block as you simultaneously counter with a straight-line punch (see page 48).

PUSHING-HANDS

Strictly speaking, the pushing-hands technique is not actually a way to block, but practicing it does develop good defensive skills. In the pushing-hands technique, force is passed from one hand to the other; this is done to test the practitioner's state of mind, physical balance, and reflexes. In pushing-hands, avoid "struggling" with force; rather, it is important to harmonize with forces by blending with them, neutralizing them, and returning them to the sender.

Pushing-hands methods include pushing and changing hands, pressing and trapping hands, escaping hands, rolling arms, gripping hands, grip escapes, leg traps, leg presses, leg escapes, advancing, retreating, and circle stepping; all of these methods are practiced in combat. Repetition is a part of learning to push hands, but the movement must never become routine.

KEEPING SILK

The quality of force used between pushing-hands partners is traditionally referred to as "silk." This name refers to the evenness of tension that must be maintained when spinning silk. If the tension varies, the thread will snap, the spinning will stop and start, and the finished silk will be lumpy and weak. However, if the thread tension is smoothly maintained, the spinning will be continuous and the silk will be fine, even, and strong.

Similarly, in kung fu, if force is met with force, conflict and chaos will result, with the strongest or most-aggressive person usually winning. This is low-grade kung fu, if indeed, it can be called kung fu at all. Without a clear understanding of what you are doing, pushing-hands practice can turn into a shoving match that eventually becomes a crude wrestling match. So take care to apply only proper kung fu techniques.

PUSHING-HANDS STRUCTURE

There are three distinct phases in pushing-hands practice:

1. Detect (detecting a force): Because pushing-hands is practiced with the arms in contact, its chief means of detecting an attack is by touch.

2. Cling (intercepting, sticking to, and neutralizing the force): After detecting a force, one clings to it. The motto is: "Stick to the partner's limbs, unless one of your own is trapped." If an arm is trapped, free it and at the same time, monitor your partner's free arm with your free arm. The free hand must not be taken too far from the center, because your partner will eventually begin to push there.

3. Return (redirecting the force): Return all forces by either turning at the waist; passing a force to your other hand and returning it with that hand;

PUSHING HANDS

STEP 1: Position your forearms so that the outer edge of your right arm makes contact with the outer edge of your partner's forearm.

STEP 2: Begin to turn your waist and yield to your partner's palm press or push.

soaking it up with one hand, passing it to the other hand, and then returning it with that hand; or by changing posture.

TOUCH REFLEXES

All of the pushing-hands movements depend on touch reflexes. Touch reflexes are immediate and faster than visual reflexes (feeling is quicker than looking). Touch reflexes can be executed as quickly as taking one's hand away from a hot stove. Indeed, there is no thinking through or planning such a response.

Compared with other physical faculties that can decrease by up to 90 percent as we grow older, touch reflexes are among the last of our faculties to do so. Because of the longevity of our touch reflexes and because the pushing-hands techniques operate only within the natural range

STEP 3: Once your partner's force is spent, ensure both of your arms remain in contact to monitor the situation.

STEP 4: Make sure you are in a good position to return your partner's force and push back to his or her center with a palm push of your own.

of movement, a high standard of pushing-hands skill can be maintained into old age.

EXAMPLES OF PUSHING-HANDS PRACTICE

Face your partner with your forearms in contact at approximately the height of your solar plexus. Neither practitioner should let his or her arms collapse. Taking care not to fully extend the arms, press smoothly forward towards your partner's chest. Your partner will detect the force and hold it momentarily before yielding to it by turning at the waist. Taking care not to fully extend his or her arm, he or she will then return the force in a smooth, circular, flowing action.

At an advanced level, it will become possible to practice pushing-hands while blindfolded.

Kung Fu Strikes and Kicks

There is a vast number of punching, striking, and kicking techniques available to the kung fu practitioner. The success of these techniques depends upon a foundation of good posture, clean technique, accuracy, and power.

SAFETY

One of the most important aspects of kung fu striking and kicking techniques is user safety—particularly for young people. There is no point in sustaining or even risking an injury during training; that would be counterproductive. Self-defense starts with looking after both yourself and others. This means that you should always "pull" punches, strikes, and kicks short of their targets when training with a partner. Furthermore, always make sure that your body is warmed up and that your back and legs are well stretched before engaging in any striking or kicking techniques.

Before we move on to the kicking techniques, we will look at a couple of striking techniques from the wing chun style, followed by some techniques taken from the white crane style.

This high kick fits well with the modern image of kung fu. Although it is undoubtedly impressive, please bear in mind that it is unlikely the ancient masters practiced kicks like this.

WING CHUN PUNCH

The wing chun punch has a reputation for being direct, fast, and incredibly economical. Wing chun practitioners claim it is capable of inflicting devastating damage. To practice it, keep the elbow of the punching hand tucked in and rapidly extend your arm along an imaginary midline, directly to the target.

WING CHUN STRIKES

The striking techniques of wing chun are simple. Based on the notion that the shortest distance between two points is a straight line, they consist of the vertical punch, palm-strike, three types of uppercut punch, and spear-fingers strike. Here are a few of the most commonly used wing chun and crane-style strikes.

BASIC WING CHUN PUNCH (JIK CHUNG)

This punch is focused along the center line of the body. Keep your elbow close to your body, and punch out. The bottom three knuckles make contact.

FINGER JAB (BIU TZE)

The finger jab is a speedy technique that adds extra length to a strike. The mechanics of the finger jab are similar to those of the punch. Keep your elbow in close to your centerline when using the jab.

FINGER JAB (BIU TZE)

Wing chun's famous finger strikes (biu-tze) have long been held in awe. However, we should bear in mind a wing chun maxim: "Hand against hand, foot against foot, there is no unstoppable technique."

FACING OFF

STEP 1: Traditionally, if a lengthy gap or space appears between opponents, no particular position is required, simply because they are out of reach. However, modern kung fu prefers to use specific preparatory postures.

TIBETAN LAMA WHITE CRANE LONG PUNCH

Starting from the cat stance (see page 35), swing your body sideways and attack the side of your opponent's body.

CRANE BEAK STRIKE

Starting from the cat stance (see page 35), shift to the side of your opponent to avoid his or her attack, and then hook-block the attack and

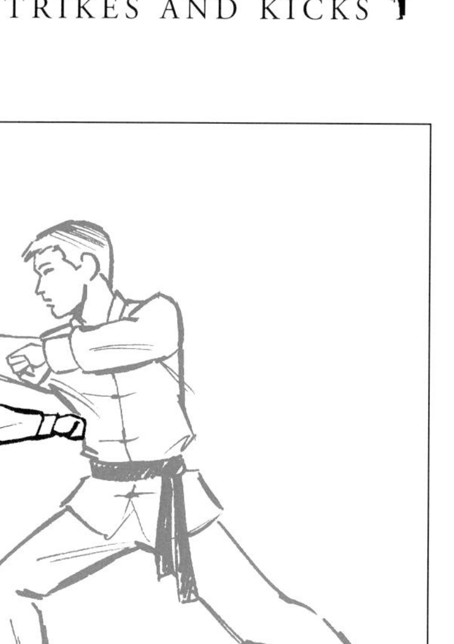

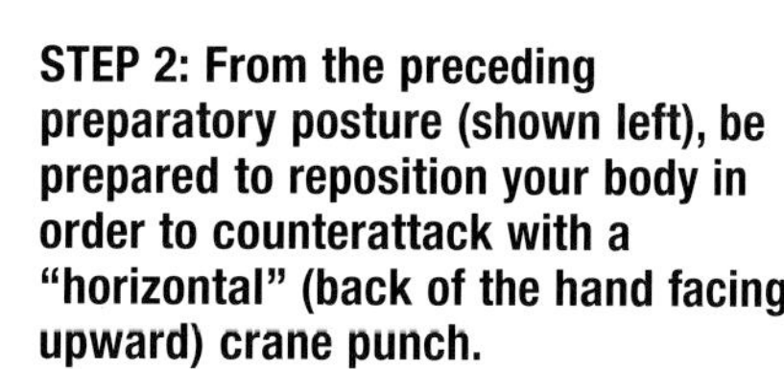

STEP 2: From the preceding preparatory posture (shown left), be prepared to reposition your body in order to counterattack with a "horizontal" (back of the hand facing upward) crane punch.

counterattack with a crane beak strike, using the bunched fingers as an anatomical weapon.

KICKING TECHNIQUES

Because the legs are stronger than the arms, kicking techniques, while slower than hand techniques, are more powerful. Modern kung fu uses a lot of kicks, while traditional kung fu uses far fewer. A selection of kung fu kicking techniques drawn from several different styles is illustrated here.

Traditional kung fu kicking techniques are directed at low targets, including the sides of the trunk and the solar plexus. The kicking leg should be pulled back as soon as possible in order to minimize the vulnerability of being on one leg. High kicks might be fun for show and may score points in competition, but some traditionalists frown upon them. If a kick is used at all, it will most likely be in conjunction with a supporting hand technique, such as a grab.

WARMING UP

The one thing you always need to keep in mind with kicking techniques is your degree of flexibility. If you are not very flexible, you may risk injury if you are too ambitious, too quick, or try high kicks without proper preparation. Remember, the most effective kicks are those that are kept within your natural range of movement. You will be no good at all in a combat situation if you overstretch yourself performing a kick and tear a muscle.

For high kicks, flexibility can be greatly improved through careful and regular stretching. If you overstretch, however, you may destabilize the muscular support in the joints, so respect your body's limits.

For practical purposes, keep kicks safe and natural. Remember, you cannot warm up, stretch, or prepare in any way before using kicks in a self-defense situation. Another word of advice: pay particular attention to the knee and hip positions during the initial and preparatory stages of all kicks.

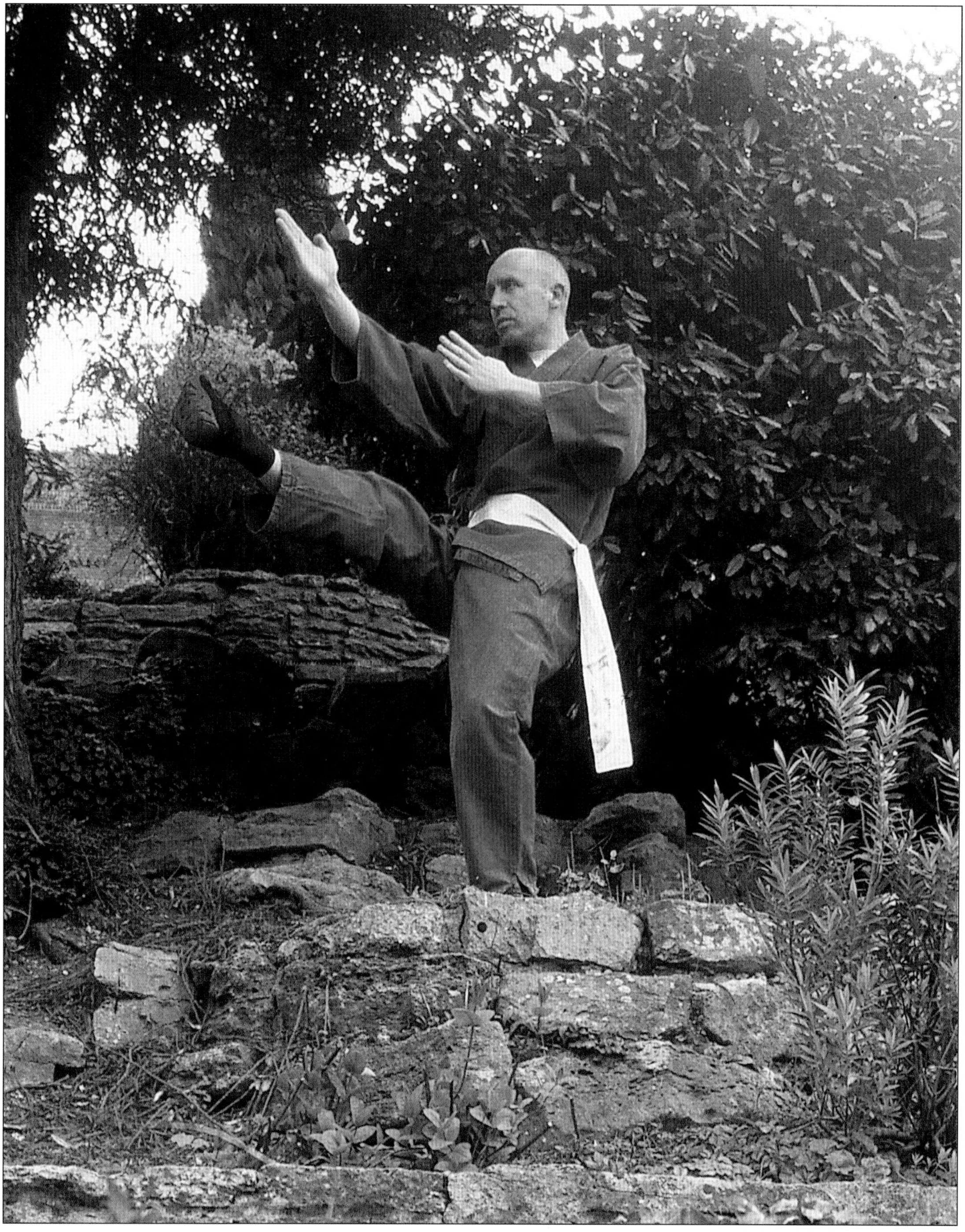

Most traditional kung fu kicking techniques, such as this front kick, are linked with a "bridging" or arm technique that seeks to destroy or at least control an opponent's balance.

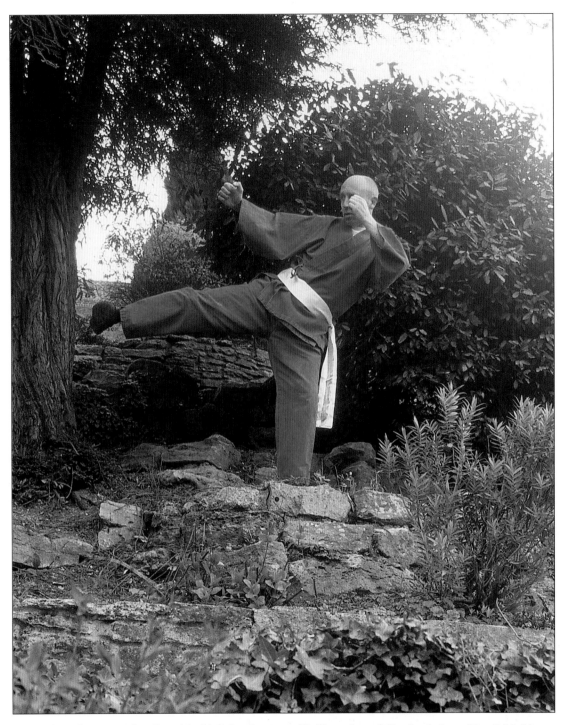

The point of contact for the side kick is always with the edge of the foot. As with all kicking techniques, the martial artist should practice until the movements become second-nature.

THE FRONT KICK

Stand in a front-leg-bent stance. Raise the knee of your kicking leg so that it is at least parallel with the floor. Make sure that the knee of the supporting, or platform, leg is well bent and that the supporting foot is pointing forward. Thrust the kicking leg out and forward while pushing the foot forward and pulling the toes back, so that if the kick were to land, it would make contact with the heel.

THE SIDE KICK

Stand in a front-leg-bent stance. Raise the knee of your kicking leg so that it is at least parallel with the floor. Make sure that the knee of the supporting, or platform, leg is well bent, and that the supporting foot is pointing sideways. Turn the hips until the thigh of the kicking leg faces the intended target and the lead hip is in a comfortable position. Thrust the kicking leg sideways and out while bending the ankle and pulling the toes back. The point of contact is with the edge of the foot.

KICKS IN FILMS

The kung fu film industry is largely, but not solely, responsible for the widespread belief that kicking techniques, particularly those aimed at high targets, are a major aspect of kung fu. In reality, traditional Chinese kung fu makes conservative use of kicking techniques and is much more concerned with close-quarters combat and the neutralizing of an opponent's attack.

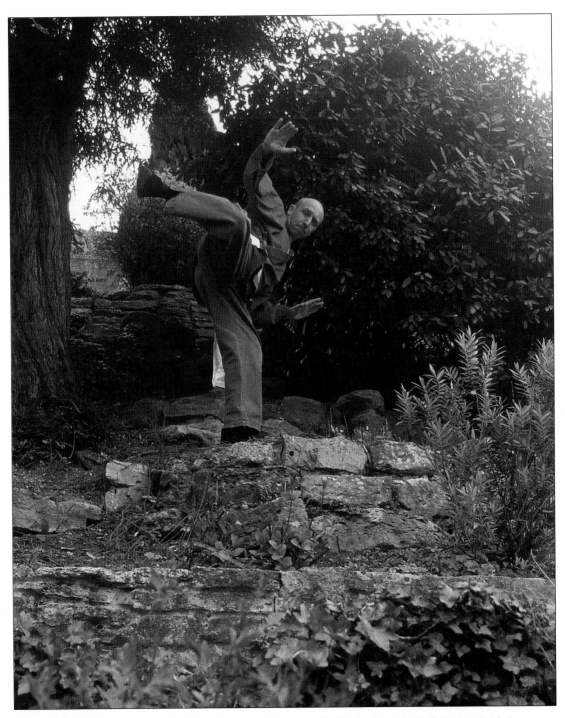

Good kung fu techniques exhibit elegance, power, and physical control. This hook kick, although not part of traditional kung fu, is still an impressive technique.

THE ROUND KICK

Stand in a front-leg-bent stance. Raise the knee of your kicking leg so that it is at least parallel with the floor. Make sure that the knee of the supporting, or platform, leg is well bent and that the supporting foot is pointing sideways. Begin to turn the hip of the kicking leg as you "flick" the leg out in a semicircle. The point of contact should be with the top of the arch or the ball of the foot.

The action of the back kick requires the practioner to turn his or her body 180 degrees.

THE BACK KICK

Stand in a front-leg-bent stance. Pivoting on the ball of your front leg, turn your body 180 degrees. Raise the knee of your kicking leg so that it is at least parallel with the floor. Make sure that the knee of the supporting, or platform, leg is well bent and that the supporting foot is pointing directly backward. Thrust the kicking leg out backward towards the target. The point of contact should be with the heel.

Sports Kung Fu

Sports kung fu, like sports karate, is a relatively modern invention. The most important element of sports kung fu is to have the correct attitude, and the correct attitude to adopt for all competing practitioners is one of sportsmanship. According to kung fu philosophy, winning is not everything and your opponent should be shown proper respect. And always bear in mind that, unlike in some films, kung fu tournaments are not life-or-death situations.

There are two types of kung fu contests or tournaments: semi-contact and full contact. In semi-contact kung fu, light, controlled blows are allowed to touch selected targets on an opponent. They must not, however, land with any force or destructive power. To land a blow with real force is to risk injury to both yourself and your opponent. To do so would also result in disqualification. For the purposes of this book, we will focus attention on semi-contact kung fu.

THE KUNG FU CONTEST

The rules for kung fu contests vary from country to country and from association to association; however, there a number of standard ones.

Two airborne combatants vie for position. Such techniques epitomize the modern image of the extraordinary powers that kung fu skills offer.

A center referee, assisted by four corner judges, normally conducts kung fu contests, and usually there is a chief referee whose decision is final. The kung fu contest area can be up to 9.5 square yards (8 sq m), but this is by no means a hard-and-fast rule. Sometimes, in the center of this square, two lines are marked 3.3 yards (3 m) apart. These lines are the fighting marks, and contestants must stay behind their respective marks until the contest begins. A judge will sit at each corner of the square with two flags, one red and one white. The flags are to signal to the center referee.

One of the contestants will wear a red sash, and one will wear a white sash. (this is not an absolute rule). These sashes have nothing to do with the contestant's actual grade or rank; they are merely worn in order to allow a clear distinction to be made between contestants. The sash colors relate to the flags carried by the judges so that points can be awarded depending upon which flag is raised.

CONTEST RULES

The contestant scores a point if he or she delivers an accurate punch, kick, or strike to a recognized target area and with enough perceived power, form, attitude, and control. A full point is often awarded for the clean delivery of a variety of techniques under the following circumstances:

- When a well-timed attack catches an advancing opponent.
- An attack delivered to an off-balance opponent.
- A combination of successive and accurate techniques.
- A takedown (foot-sweep) and punch combination.
- If an opponent loses the will to fight or turns his or her back, a

Despite their violent themes, kung fu movies generally promote the victory of good over evil, as we can see in one of the concluding scenes from Bruce Lee's famous film *Enter The Dragon*.

point can be awarded against him or her.

- An attack successfully delivered to an unguarded, legitimate target.

FORBIDDEN TECHNIQUES AND FOULS

When kung fu tournament fighting was popularized, standards of safety had to be set and implemented. These standards included a broad classification of forbidden techniques and fouls:

CRANE BLOCK AND STRIKE
Blocking and striking simultaneously is a typical tactic used in white crane kung fu.

- Direct-contact attacks to any part of the body, except the upper and lower limbs.
- Direct contact to joints.
- Persistent attacks to the shins to break morale or intimidate.
- Attacks to the eyes or privates.
- Unnecessary or excessive body grabbing and clinching.
- The use of knife-hand or spear-finger strikes.
- Wasting time or leaving the arena too frequently.
- Verbal abuse or provocation.

CONTEST SCORING

The contest scoring method is most commonly found in multidiscipline tournaments. It is derived from modern karate contests:

- For a full point, the judge raises the flag higher than the shoulder.
- For a half point, the judge raises the flag lower than the shoulder.
- If the judge sees a foul or thinks a contestant should be disqualified, he or she turns the relevant flag several times above his or her head.
- If the judge sees no score after a clash of contestants, he or she waves both flags right and left, crossing them just above the knees.
- If the judge did not see the clash of techniques at all, he or she momentarily covers both eyes with the flags.
- If the judge is certain that both contestants scored at the same time, he or she points the ends of each flag toward each other in front of the chest.

If no full score has been made at the end of a contest, the referee will call for the judges' decision. The judges will then raise the red or white flag, depending upon which contestant they think has won. If a judge feels that the contest should be a draw, he or she crosses both flags above the head.

A contestant leading the contest with a half-point score will not automatically win. If it is felt that he or she has been backpedaling and avoiding his or her opponent in order to cling to the marginal lead, he or she will lose the contest. The referee has the power to overrule one judge, but if two or more judges want to award a point, it is usually awarded.

Kung Fu Weapons

Modern kung fu draws on the 18 classical weapons of China. It makes use of them in various ways and for various reasons, ranging from military to keeping fit, and from competition to demonstration.

A HISTORY OF KUNG FU WEAPONS

In his book, *The Sword Polishers Record the Way of Kung Fu*, kung fu teacher and author Adam Hsu talks about the weapons of the Shaolin Temple. "The most famous weapon of the Shaolin Temple was the staff. This fact helps to illustrate that Shaolin was a Buddhist school. No actual weapons were kept in the temple. Machine guns and missiles are not stored in churches; likewise, weapons were not stored in a Buddhist temple. The most famous weapon practiced at Shaolin was the staff, because it was the only weapon available to the monks."

The following story, taken from a book called *Barefoot Zen*, supports this understanding. On one occasion, Chu asked Master Li Tsun Ya about the weapons that lined the Eighteen Lohan Hall. "How could Buddhist monks who practiced the perfections of the tripitaka (the original teachings of the Buddha) possibly countenance the use of weapons?" Master Li smiled and replied, "The so-called weapons that you see lining

Here we see a typical defensive maneuver using a trident, a kind of three-pronged spear, one of several ancient (and dramatic) Chinese weapons now associated with kung fu.

A WORD OF CAUTION

These weapons can be dangerous! As such, you are strongly advised not to attempt to use them without receiving proper instruction and supervision.

the Eighteen Lohan Hall are only for ritual use. Our monks manipulate these large ceremonial staffs symbolically, like a parade master wields a baton. Their use is completely symbolic. The staves are far too cumbersome, hefty, and impractical to be used as actual weapons. Besides, to attempt such a thing would bring disgrace upon us. Would it be a worthy trade, that of living with weapons instead of living the teachings of the Buddha? We only use these objects during ritual and festive occasions."

Chinese weapons have a long history. They include the **broadsword** (a flat-bladed, single-edged sword); the straight double-edged sword (popular with tai chi practitioners); the double-edged **butterfly knives** (popular with wing chun stylists); the spear; the two-sectional staff (best known as **nunchakas**) made popular by Bruce Lee in the movie *Enter the Dragon*; and the three-sectional staff, which is similar to the nunchakas, but consists of three divisions rather than two.

These and other weapons formed part of the military's arsenal—as well as that of some common people—in ancient China. Horsemanship and archery were also used in ancient Chinese warfare. Needless to say, all of these weapons lost their significance and importance during the Ching

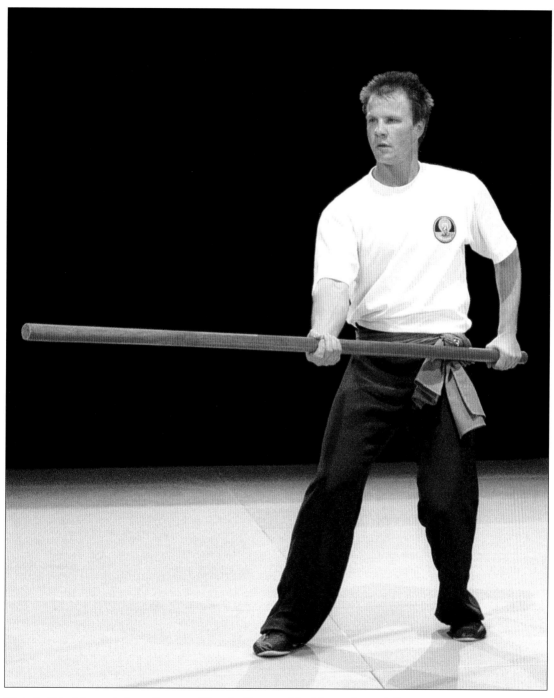

The staff holds an interesting position in the world of kung fu and its weapons because Shaolin monks were permitted to own a staff for walking. It is possible that they used the staff in various "contact" routines, like pushing-hands.

Dynasty (1644–1912), when the use of gunpowder became essential to waging successful modern warfare.

TYPES OF CHINESE WEAPONS

There are two distinctions that need to be made between the different types of Chinese weapons: the Shaolin staff, or pole, is classed as one type of weapon, while those weapons with a cutting edge belong in a separate category. There are four basic divisions of Chinese weapons today: the staff (which was described earlier), the spear, the broadsword, and the straight sword.

THE SPEAR

The Chinese spear is sometimes referred to as the king of kung fu weapons. It is 8 to 10 feet long, with a pointed metal end that is often decorated with feather plumes. The techniques for using the spear were once a model of simplicity. In fact, legend has it that General Chi (a famous general who fought during the Ming Dynasty) only taught his troops two techniques: the jab and the strike-down.

More recently, spear techniques have become more complex and subtle, and are difficult to master. This is due mostly to the fact that the spear is now a competition and demonstration tool rather than a weapon of war. Following are some spear techniques taught by coaches at the Beijing Physical Culture Institute.

Left: Use of the spear in kung fu is unquestionably a technique that was developed outside and beyond the confines of Shaolin kung fu. Modern wu shu spear techniques like this are dramatic rather than practical.

THE UPWARD SPEAR STRIKE

STEP 1: Following a straight thrust, keep the left hand extended.

STEP 2: Loosen the grip on the spear and pull the bottom of the spear down to the hip with the right hand.

STEP 3: Slide the spear through the left hand. The downward pull of the right hand causes the spear to strike up.

THE UPWARD SPEAR STRIKE

In this technique, the spear is used following a straight thrust. To perform this strike, keep the left hand extended. Loosen the grip on the spear, and then pull the bottom of the spear down to the hip with the right hand. Slide the spear through the left hand. The downward pull of the right hand causes the spear to strike up.

THE BROADSWORD

There are many postures that one can use with the broadsword. Four of the most popular are the lifting-the-leg-to-pierce posture, the drift-with-the-current posture, and the turning-the-sword-to-pierce postures (there are two postures with this name).

THE STRAIGHT SWORD

One technique for the straight sword is called "big dipper," which is an exotic name for a subtle counterattacking technique.

KUNG FU AS ENTERTAINMENT

Kung fu movies are popular with both Western and Eastern audiences. The origin of these movies is a mixture of Chinese culture, politics, and the kung fu myths and legends of the Ming (1368–1644) and Ching (1644–1912) dynasties. Add a dash of Hollywood, and you have some exciting movies.

However, kung fu was used as form of entertainment even before anyone made movies. Throughout the centuries, kung fu techniques were adapted by touring troops of entertainers and used to illustrate stories,

The character Kwai Chang Cain played by U.S. actor David Carradine in the T.V. series *Kung Fu*, inspired a generation of martial artists. The series stressed the philosophy and beauty of kung fu rather than the violence.

BROADSWORD POSTURES

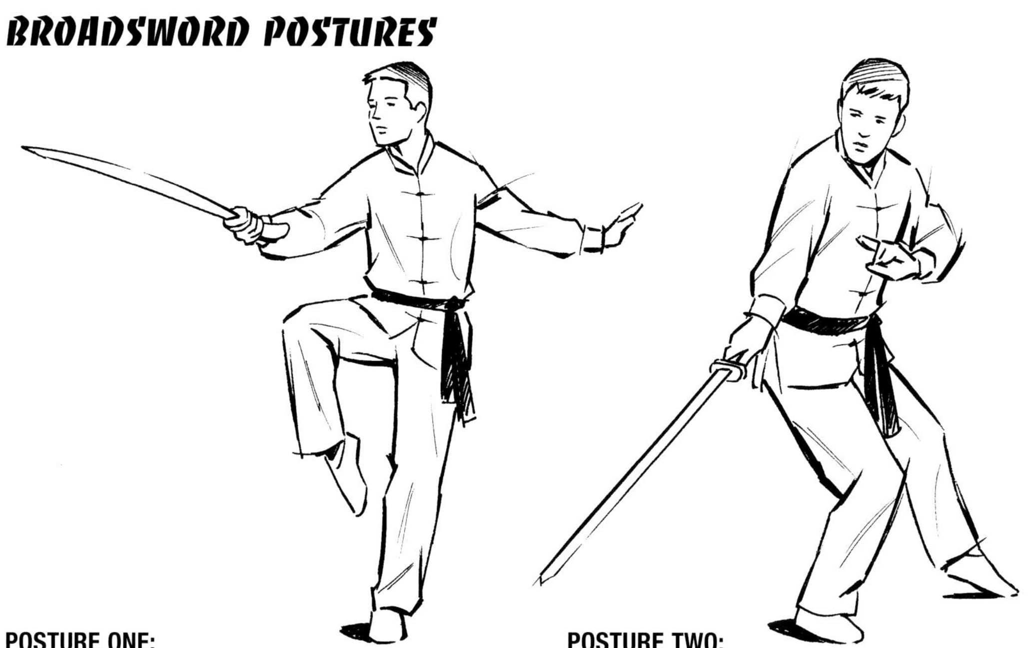

POSTURE ONE:
"Lift the leg" posture is used with a broadsword, to "lunge" while withdrawing, or prior to lunging forward with a strike.

POSTURE TWO:
"Drift with the current" posture is a straight-sword "attitude" that can be used for attack or defense.

POSTURE THREE:
"Turning the sword to pierce" (version 1) is a "riposte." The sword is used to deflect, then the blade is quickly turned for a counterattack.

POSTURE FOUR:
"Turning the sword to pierce" (version 2) posture is arguably a distraction technique.

Buddhist monks and nuns never drink alcohol, but the film title *Shaolin Drunken Monk* provides a good example of the tall stories often associated with Shaolin kung fu.

bringing them to life and making them more entertaining. This is easier than it sounds, however, as the players in ancient Chinese traveling theaters had to be understood all over China. This was no mean feat, considering the number of different languages and dialects spoken throughout this vast country. The audience had to get the point of a particular scene or action, or they might become bored. This meant a reliance on facial expressions, props, and lots of action, so that even if the words were not clear to a particular audience, they could at least understand what was going on because of the exaggerated acting style. Kung fu films retain this exaggerated acting element to this day, and it has now become both accepted and expected.

Kung fu movies often have revenge as a theme. They are usually full of vengeful heroes fighting Shaolin monks and nuns and supernatural beings. Shaolin monks and nuns were famed for their healing abilities, particularly during the Ming Dynasty (1368–1644). They were also martial artists, as

WARNING

Some of the scenes in kung fu movies depict extreme violence. Check the film classification if you are uncertain about the contents of a film, and remember: what is shown in kung fu films is for entertainment only. These films do not represent the depth and majesty of authentic Chinese kung fu.

well as religious hermits, but they were not the type of kung fu "hero" commonly seen in the movies. The origin of the myth of the kung fu avenging hero can most likely be traced back to the Fong Sai Yuk legends, which began after the fall of the Ming Dynasty in 1644.

Fong Sai Yuk was the prototypical hero for the kung fu films from the late 1960s onwards. He was the legendary avenging hero of the **Han** Chinese struggle against their **Manchu** oppressors. During the period after the fall of the Ming Dynasty and the burning of the Shaolin Temple, the previously monastic kung fu went public, and Fong Sai Yuk became the Arnold Schwarzenegger of his time.

Patriotic societies soon arose from the ashes of the Manchu destruction of the Shaolin Temple, and the **fist-in-the-palm** kung fu salutation came into use at this time. It was used as a greeting, but it also had a political meaning: "Overthrow the Ching (the non-native Manchu) Dynasty and restore the Ming (the native Han) Dynasty."

These patriotic societies later became the Triad, or gangster groups, and in this political climate, many kung fu styles received their names. These are just some of the events that converged to provide a rich, dramatic backdrop for the emerging kung fu films.

MODERN KUNG FU STARS

Undoubtedly, the best-known Chinese kung fu stars of the 20th and 21st centuries are Bruce Lee and Jackie Chan. Both performers have thrilled audiences for many years, yet both have completely different approaches and screen images: Lee often plays the avenging hero, whereas Chan usually plays a hapless hero. Furthermore, a strong vein of Chinese opera and acrobatics flows through many Chan movies, whereas Lee movies tend to be darker.

The exploits of a collection of semimythical figures, including the Monkey King and a Buddhist monk, made for a long-running TV series during the 1980s, in which Chinese martial arts and mythology were mixed together. The stars were Japanese, and the program was called *Monkey*.

JACKIE CHAN

Jackie Chan was born on April 17, 1954. His original name was Chan Kong-sang. His family came from Shantung Province in China. When Chan was seven years old, his parents emigrated to Australia and enrolled Chan at The China Drama Academy.

During his early period of study at the academy, Chan and six fellow students starred as the "Seven Cute Kids" in a series of kung fu comedies. At the age of eight, he made his first screen appearance in a Cantonese film called *Big and Little Wong Tin-Bar*. This led to a series of child roles. By the age of 15, however, he was too big for child roles, so he began to work as a stunt man, doing such things as diving off roofs—all for just $15 a day.

If you were Jackie Chan's stuntman, you would have little work to do since Chan does most of his own (often dangerous) stunts.

Later, he began to choreograph fight scenes, and eventually, Chan was offered some small character roles, mostly as the second male lead. In 1973, he got his first break as a leading man in the film *Little Tiger of Guandong*. Then, in 1978, Seasonal Films borrowed Chan to star in the kung fu film that made a name for him: *Snake in the Eagle's Shadow*. It was a massive box-office success, making Chan a superstar overnight. This film followed the classic revenge theme mentioned earlier, but Chan's unique blend of comedy, spectacular martial arts skills, and acrobatics became his trademark.

Chan followed up on the success of *Snake in the Eagle's Shadow* with a film called *Drunken Master*. It became the highest-grossing martial arts film in Hong Kong. In 1980, Chan emerged on the Hollywood scene with the film *Battlecreek Brawl*.

BRUCE LEE

Bruce Lee was born on November 27, 1940, in San Francisco. His given name was Lee Jun-Fan. His parents were from Hong Kong. At the time of his birth, Lee's father was involved in a theatrical tour of the U.S. When the tour ended, the family returned to Hong Kong, where Lee grew up.

Despite being Hong Kong's cha-cha dance champion, Lee liked to fight, and began to study kung fu in order to gain an advantage over other boys. Lee had a friend named William Cheung who had a reputation for always winning his fights. Cheung was a practitioner of wing chun kung fu and a student of its grandmaster, Yip Man.

Yip Man taught in a traditional way. Classes were small and not particularly well-organized. Lee began to take Yip's classes, later recalling that he suffered bruising when he did sticking-hands with his friend Cheung. Lee went on to found the jeet kune do style of kung fu, which is based on wing chun (see page 45).

Right: This famous pose is actually from the film *Karate Kid*. It shows a (Hollywood version) of a white crane kung fu technique that found its way into karate styles.

Bruce Lee turned the "nunchaka," a previously obscure martial arts weapon, into a well-known and now mass-produced weapon. In fact, the nunchaka started life as a rural agricultural tool used to thresh grain.

In his youth, Lee acted in several films and wanted to become a professional actor, but his mother would not let him. When he was 18, he was shipped off to San Francisco to stay with family friends. He later moved to Seattle, where he worked at Ruby Chow's Chinese restaurant. Later, Lee enrolled at Edison High School to complete his education, and then went on to enroll at the University of Washington.

In late 1959, Lee took part in a kung fu demonstration in Seattle. While there, he met Jesse Glover, a famous American sports personality, who asked him for instruction in kung fu. This led to the formation of a small school of kung fu headed by Lee.

But Lee never gave up on his acting. During the 1960s, Lee appeared in a television program called *Longstreet*, and later, in a series called *The Green Hornet*. In 1971, Lee's first film, *The Big Boss* (filmed in Thailand), broke all box-office records. Lee went on to make *The Fists of Fury*, *Way of the Dragon*, and *Enter The Dragon*. His career came to a tragic halt when he died unexpectedly on July 20, 1973.

JIMMY WANG YU

Disability in martial arts occurs in the legend of a one-armed Buddhist nun proficient in kung fu and the famous depiction of a one-armed kung fu hero in the film *One Armed Boxer* released in the 1960s and starring Jimmy Wang Yu, who, up until the advent of the Bruce Lee movies, was a popular star with Asian audiences.

Glossary

Broadsword A flat Chinese sword with a curved blade

Buddha hand An open-handed defensive posture and also the name of a kung fu style

Chi Vital breath or spirit

Fist-in-the-palm A traditional Chinese greeting

Han Chinese dynasty which ruled from 206 B.C. to A.D. 220

Judo The gentle way; a Japanese martial art that utilizes throwing and grappling techniques

Karate "Empty hands"; a Japanese martial art that uses punching, blocking, kicking, striking, and grappling techniques

Manchu People of northeastern China, founders of the Qing Dynasty (1644–1912)

Mime The theatrical art of conveying meaning without words using gestures and facial expressions

Sifu "Father-teacher"; a traditional title for a kung fu teacher

Sticking-hands A type of reflex training used by kung fu students

White crane A traditional Southern Chinese martial arts style or group of styles

Clothing and Equipment

CLOTHING

Gi: The gi is the most typical martial arts "uniform." Usually in white, but also available in other colors, it consists of a cotton thigh-length jacket and calf-length trousers. Gis come in three weights: light, medium, and heavy. Lightweight gis are cooler than heavyweight gis, but not as strong. The jacket is usually bound at the waist with a belt.

Belt: Belts are used in the martial arts to denote the rank and experience of the wearer. They are made from strong linen or cotton and wrap several times around the body before tying. Beginners usually wear a white belt, and the final belt is almost always black.

Hakama: A long folded skirt with five pleats at the front and one at the back. It is a traditional form of clothing in kendo, iaido, and jujutsu.

Zori: A simple pair of slip-on sandals worn in the dojo when not training to keep the floor clean.

WEAPONS

Bokken: A bokken is a long wooden sword made from Japanese oak. Bokken are roughly the same size and shape as a traditional Japanese sword (katana).

Jo: The jo is a simple wooden staff about 4–5 ft (1.3–1.6 m) long and is a traditional weapon of karate and aikido.

Kamma: Two short-handled sickles used as a fighting tool in some types of karate and jujutsu.
Tanto: A wooden knife used for training purposes.
Hojo jutsu: A long rope with a noose on one end used in jujutsu to restrain attackers.
Sai: Long, thin, and sharp spikes, held like knives and featuring wide, spiked handguards just above the handles.
Tonfa: Short poles featuring side handles, like modern-day police batons.
Katana: A traditional Japanese sword with a slightly curved blade and a single, razor-sharp cutting edge.
Butterfly knives: A pair of knives, each one with a wide blade. They are used mainly in kung fu.
Nunchaku: A flail-like weapon consisting of three short sections of staff connected by chains.
Shinai: A bamboo training sword used in the martial art of kendo.
Iaito: A stainless-steel training sword with a blunt blade used in the sword-based martial art of iaido.

TRAINING AIDS

Mook yan jong: A wooden dummy against which the martial artist practices his blocks and punches and conditions his limbs for combat.
Makiwara: A plank of wood set in the ground used for punching and kicking practice.
Focus pads: Circular pads worn on the hands by one person, while his or her partner uses the pads for training accurate punching.

PROTECTIVE EQUIPMENT

Headguard: A padded, protective helmet that protects the wearer from blows to the face and head.

Joint supports: Tight foam or bandage sleeves that go around elbow, knee, or ankle joints and protect the muscles and joints against damage during training.

Groin protector: A well-padded undergarment for men that protects the testicles and the abdomen from kicks and low punches.

Practice mitts: Lightweight boxing gloves that protect the wearer's hands from damage in sparring, and reduce the risk of cuts being inflicted on the opponent.

Chest protector: A sturdy shield worn by women over the chest to protect the breasts during sparring.

Further Reading

Chow, David and Richard Spangler. *Kung Fu: History, Philosophy, and Technique.* Burbank, CA: Unique Publications, 1989.

Chye Khim, P'Ng and Don F. Draeger. *Shaolin Lohan Kung-Fu.* Boston: Charles E. Tuttle Co,1991.

Hallander, Jane. *The Complete Guide to Kung Fu Fighting Styles.* Burbank, CA: Unique Publications, 1985.

Liang, Shou-Yu and Wen-Ching Wu. *Kung Fu Elements: Wushu Training and Martial Arts Application Manual.* East Providence, RI: Way of the Dragon Publishing, 2001.

Miao, Jiawen. *The Tao of Health and Fitness: The Kung-Fu Master's Workout.* Burbank, CA: Unique Publications, 2000.

Shum, Leung. *The Secrets of Eagle Claw Kung Fu: Ying Jow Pai.* Boston: Charles E. Tuttle Co, 2001.

Wong, Doc-Fai and Jane Hallander. *Shaolin Five Animals.* Burbank, CA: Unique Publications, 1987.

Useful Web Sites

http://martialarts.org/

http://www.kungFu.net/

http://www.yingjowpai.net/

http://www.moyyat.com/

http://www.tigercrane.com/

http://www.pa-kua.com/

http://www.kungfu-wusu.com/

http://www.shaolin.com/

About the Author

Nathan Johnson holds a 6th-dan black belt in karate and a 4th-degree black sash in traditional Chinese kung fu. He has studied martial arts for 30 years and holds seminars and lectures on martial arts and related subjects throughout the world. He teaches zen shorindo karate at several leading universities in the U.K. His previous books include *Zen Shaolin Karate* and *Barefoot Zen.* He lives in Hampshire, England.

Index

References in italics refer to illustration captions